A book of yoga symbols, waiting to be filled
With colors that breathe life into each illustrated field
As we turn the pages, a journey unfolds
A path to mindfulness, a story to be told

The lotus flower, with petals open wide
A symbol of enlightenment, a guide to our inside
We color it in shades of pink and white
And feel a sense of peace, a state of light

The Om symbol, a sound that resonates
Through our minds and bodies, as we meditate
We color it in vibrant shades of blue
And feel its power, as it guides us through

The sun and moon, in perfect harmony
A symbol of balance, a yin and yang journey
We color them in golden and silver hues
And feel the balance within, a sense of renewed

As we color each symbol, we learn and we grow
A journey of self-discovery, a chance to glow
For in each stroke of color, we find a way
To connect with ourselves, to find peace each day.

with love, Selah Moon

MANDALA

Mandala is a geometric design that represents the universe and serves as a spiritual and ritual symbol in Hinduism and Buddhism. The term "mandala" comes from Sanskrit, meaning "circle" or "center," and refers to the circular shape of the design.

Mandalas typically feature a central point, with various patterns and shapes radiating outwards in a circular pattern. They are often created using colored sand, paint, or other materials, and can range from simple designs to intricate and detailed patterns.

In yoga and meditation, mandalas are often used as a tool for concentration and visualization. Practitioners may focus their gaze on the center of the mandala and use it as a focal point for their meditation, or visualize themselves as the central point of the mandala and explore the patterns and shapes radiating outwards.

Mandalas are also believed to have healing properties and are used in various forms of therapy and self-care practices. Creating or coloring mandalas is said to promote relaxation, reduce stress and anxiety, and enhance creativity and mindfulness.

THE MANDALA SYMBOLIZES THE INFINITE UNIVERSE AND THE INTERCONNECTEDNESS OF ALL THINGS, REMINDING US OF OUR PLACE IN THE COSMIC WEB OF EXISTENCE.

BUDDHA

Buddha, also known as Siddhartha Gautama, was an ancient Indian sage and philosopher who founded Buddhism.

According to traditional accounts, Buddha was born into a royal family in the 6th century BCE in what is now Nepal. He lived a life of luxury until the age of 29, when he renounced his privileged existence and set out on a spiritual quest to find the meaning of life and the path to liberation from suffering.

His teachings emphasize the importance of mindfulness, compassion, and non-attachment, which are principles that are also emphasized in yoga. In fact, many of the teachings and practices of yoga, such as meditation and self-awareness, are closely aligned with Buddhist principles. Yoga and Buddhism both seek to cultivate a sense of inner peace and harmony, and both emphasize the importance of self-discovery and personal growth.

Many modern yoga practitioners draw inspiration from Buddha's teachings and incorporate them into their practice. For example, some yoga classes may incorporate Buddhist chants or readings as part of their spiritual practice. Additionally, some yoga retreats may include Buddhist teachings or meditation practices as part of their programming.

THE PRACTICE OF YOGA
TEACHES US TO LET GO
OF ATTACHMENTS AND
FIND INNER PEACE
THROUGH DETACHMENT.

OM

Om is a sacred sound and spiritual symbol in Hinduism, Buddhism, Jainism, and Sikhism. It is considered to be the primordial sound from which the entire universe originated, and is often chanted or used as a mantra in meditation and yoga practices.

The sound of Om is said to represent the ultimate reality and consciousness of the universe, and is made up of three distinct sounds: A, U, and M. These sounds correspond to the three states of consciousness: waking, dreaming, and deep sleep, respectively.

The chanting of Om is believed to have a calming and centering effect on the mind and body, and can promote relaxation and focus during meditation and yoga practices. It is also said to stimulate the chakras and promote spiritual growth and self-awareness.

In addition to its spiritual significance, Om is also used as a decorative element in various forms of art and design. It is often depicted in the form of a symbol, which consists of the Sanskrit letters arranged in a specific way to form a visually striking image.

THE OM SYMBOL REPRESENTS THE UNITY AND INTERCONNECTEDNESS OF ALL THINGS, REMINDING US THAT WE ARE ALL ONE AND THAT OUR ACTIONS HAVE AN IMPACT ON THE WORLD AROUND US.

LOTUS

The lotus is a sacred flower in many Eastern cultures and is often associated with spiritual enlightenment, purity, and rebirth. It is particularly significant in Buddhism and Hinduism, where it is often used as a symbol in religious art, mythology, and spiritual practices.

One of the reasons why the lotus is so revered is because it grows in muddy water but emerges as a beautiful and pure flower. This represents the idea that individuals can overcome the challenges and obstacles of life and emerge as something beautiful and pure.

In Buddhism, the lotus is often associated with the Buddha himself, who is said to have been born from a lotus flower. It is also a symbol of the path to enlightenment, with each petal of the lotus representing a step on the path towards spiritual awakening.

In Hinduism, the lotus is often associated with the god Vishnu and the goddess Lakshmi. It is also a symbol of the chakras, or energy centers, in the body. The lotus flower is believed to represent the crown chakra, which is associated with enlightenment and spiritual connection.

THE LOTUS FLOWER GROWS IN THE MUD, YET STILL MANAGES TO RISE ABOVE AND BLOOM, REMINDING US OF OUR OWN POTENTIAL FOR GROWTH AND TRANSFORMATION.

NAMASTE

Namaste is a word commonly used in yoga and meditation practices. It is a Sanskrit word that has both a literal and a deeper, spiritual meaning.

Literally, the word namaste is made up of two Sanskrit words: "namah" (meaning "bow" or "obeisance") and "te" (meaning "to you"). Together, they create the simple greeting, "namaste," which is often translated as "I bow to you." However, the deeper meaning of namaste goes beyond a simple greeting. In many cultures, it is considered to be a symbol of respect, gratitude, and unity. It is a way of recognizing and honoring the divine spark within each individual.

When saying namaste, one often places their hands in prayer position at the heart center, bows the head, and says the word with a feeling of reverence and gratitude. This gesture is called "anjali mudra" and is often used in yoga as a way of bringing the hands and heart together in a gesture of respect and devotion.

In addition to being a greeting, namaste is also used as a closing to many yoga and meditation practices. It is a way of acknowledging and honoring the teacher and the teachings, as well as the other practitioners in the class.

THE PRACTICE OF YOGA TEACHES US TO LET GO OF JUDGMENT AND FIND ACCEPTANCE AND COMPASSION FOR OURSELVES AND OTHERS.

NAMASTE

HAMSA

Hamsa, also known as the Hand of Fatima or Hand of Miriam, is a symbol that originated in the Middle East and North Africa. It is a hand-shaped amulet or talisman that is often used in jewelry, wall hangings, and other decorative items.

The word hamsa comes from the Arabic word "khamsa," which means "five." The five fingers of the hand represent the five senses and the five elements (earth, air, fire, water, and ether) in Hinduism.

In yoga, the hamsa is often associated with protection, good luck, and warding off negative energy. It is believed to offer spiritual and physical protection, and is used as a symbol of peace and harmony.

In some traditions, the hamsa is also associated with the goddess Lakshmi, the Hindu goddess of wealth, fortune, and prosperity. The hand is sometimes depicted with an eye in the center, which is believed to offer protection against the evil eye.

THE PRACTICE OF YOGA
TEACHES US TO BE
PRESENT IN THE MOMENT,
TO LET GO OF WORRIES
ABOUT THE PAST AND
FUTURE AND FIND PEACE
IN THE PRESENT.

NUMBER 108

The number 108 is considered a sacred number in many cultures, including in yoga. It is said to have spiritual significance and is often used in yoga practices and rituals.

In yoga, the number 108 is believed to represent the universe's wholeness and completeness. It is said that there are 108 energy lines that converge at the heart chakra, and chanting or reciting a mantra 108 times is believed to activate these energy lines and help bring the practitioner into a state of greater awareness and spiritual connection.

The significance of the number 108 can also be seen in the following ways:

- There are 108 beads on a mala (a traditional string of prayer beads used in meditation and mantra practice).
- The distance between the sun and the Earth is roughly 108 times the sun's diameter.
- The diameter of the moon is roughly 108 times smaller than the diameter of the sun.
- In some traditions, there are 108 sacred sites in India.

THE BREATH IS A REMINDER OF THE LIFE FORCE THAT FLOWS THROUGH US ALL, CONNECTING US TO EACH OTHER AND TO THE UNIVERSE ITSELF.

108

GANESHA

Ganesha, also known as Ganapati, Vinayaka, or Pillaiyar, is one of the most beloved deities in Hinduism. He is known as the Lord of Beginnings and the Remover of Obstacles and is revered as the god of wisdom, knowledge, and new beginnings.

Ganesha is often depicted as a chubby, elephant-headed god with a round belly and a playful demeanor. His elephant head symbolizes wisdom, and his trunk represents the ability to overcome obstacles. In his four hands, he holds a variety of objects, including a conch shell, a lotus flower, and an axe.

In yoga, Ganesha is often invoked at the beginning of a practice to help remove any obstacles or challenges that may be hindering progress. He is also believed to bring good fortune, prosperity, and success to those who seek his help.

Ganesha is a beloved figure in many cultures and is celebrated in festivals and ceremonies around the world. His image can be found in temples, homes, and public spaces, and his teachings continue to inspire and uplift people of all ages and backgrounds.

YOGA IS NOT ABOUT TOUCHING YOUR TOES, IT IS ABOUT WHAT YOU LEARN ON THE WAY DOWN.

MALA

A mala is a traditional string of prayer beads that is commonly used in meditation and mantra practice in many spiritual traditions, including in yoga. The word "mala" means "garland" in Sanskrit, and the beads are often strung together with a tassel or other decorative element at the end.

A mala typically consists of 108 beads, which is a sacred number in many cultures and is believed to represent the universe's wholeness and completeness. There are also smaller versions of malas, such as wrist malas, which have 27 or 21 beads.

Malas can be made from a variety of materials, including gemstones, wood, bone, or seeds. Each type of material is believed to have different healing properties and energy, and practitioners may choose a mala based on their personal preferences and intentions.

In yoga, malas are often used in mantra practice and meditation to help focus the mind and promote a deeper spiritual connection. The practitioner will hold the mala and recite a mantra or affirmation 108 times, moving one bead at a time with each repetition.

THE PRACTICE OF YOGA
TEACHES US TO
APPROACH LIFE WITH A
SENSE OF CURIOSITY AND
EXPLORATION, AND TO
FIND JOY IN THE
JOURNEY.

FLOWER OF LIFE

The Flower of Life is a geometric pattern consisting of overlapping circles arranged in a flower-like pattern. It is considered a sacred symbol and has been found in many ancient cultures and traditions, including in Hinduism, Buddhism, and ancient Egypt.

The Flower of Life is believed to represent the underlying structure of the universe and the interconnectedness of all living things. It is said to contain the patterns of creation and the blueprint of the universe, and meditating on the symbol is believed to help promote spiritual growth and understanding. In yoga and meditation, the Flower of Life is often used as a focal point for visualization and concentration. Practitioners may visualize the symbol in their mind's eye or use a physical representation, such as a piece of jewelry or a painting, to help deepen their practice.

The Flower of Life has also been used in various healing practices, including in crystal healing and color therapy, and is believed to promote balance, harmony, and spiritual growth.

THE BREATH IS THE
FOUNDATION OF YOGA,
TEACHING US TO BE
MINDFUL OF THE PRESENT
MOMENT AND FIND INNER
PEACE THROUGH THE
RHYTHM OF OUR OWN
BREATH.

YIN YANG

The Yin Yang symbol, also known as the Taijitu, is a fundamental concept in Taoist philosophy and Chinese culture. The symbol consists of a circle divided into two halves, with one half black (Yin) and the other white (Yang), and a small dot of the opposite color in each half.

Yin represents the feminine, receptive, and passive aspects of nature, while Yang represents the masculine, active, and assertive aspects. The two halves of the circle are interconnected, and together they represent the concept of balance and harmony between opposing forces.

In yoga, the Yin Yang symbol is often used to represent the complementary nature of different yoga styles and practices. For example, Yin Yoga is a slow and gentle practice that focuses on passive stretching and relaxation, while Yang Yoga, such as Vinyasa or Power Yoga, is more active and focuses on strength and movement.

The Yin Yang symbol can also be used as a reminder to cultivate balance and harmony in one's life, both on and off the mat. By embracing both Yin and Yang qualities, individuals can find a sense of wholeness and completeness, and promote overall well-being.

YIN YANG IS A REMINDER
THAT EVEN IN THE MIDST
OF CHAOS, WE CAN FIND
BALANCE AND HARMONY
BY EMBRACING BOTH THE
LIGHT AND THE DARK
WITHIN OURSELVES.

GYAN MUDRA

The Gyan Mudra, also known as the Chin Mudra, is a hand gesture or seal commonly used in yoga and meditation. It is formed by touching the tip of the index finger to the tip of the thumb, while the other three fingers remain extended.

The Gyan Mudra is believed to help improve concentration, memory, and wisdom. It is also said to stimulate the brain and nervous system, reduce stress and anxiety, and enhance clarity and intuition.

In yoga, the Gyan Mudra is often used during meditation and pranayama (breathing exercises) to help focus the mind and cultivate a deeper awareness of the present moment. It can also be used during asana practice to help deepen the connection between the mind and body.

The Gyan Mudra is considered a powerful and simple tool for promoting inner peace, clarity, and spiritual growth. By using this hand gesture regularly, individuals can help calm the mind, reduce stress and anxiety, and promote a deeper sense of inner peace and well-being.

THE PRACTICE OF YOGA
TEACHES US TO FIND JOY
AND GRATITUDE IN THE
SIMPLE THINGS IN LIFE,
AND TO APPRECIATE THE
BEAUTY THAT SURROUNDS
US IN EVERY MOMENT.

SHRI YANTRA

The Shri Yantra is a sacred geometric symbol in Hinduism and Tantra. The Shri Yantra is often described as the "queen of all yantras" and is considered one of the most powerful and auspicious yantras.

The Shri Yantra consists of nine interlocking triangles that surround a central point, or bindu. The triangles are arranged in such a way that they form 43 smaller triangles, each with a specific meaning and symbolism. The central point, or bindu, represents the highest point of consciousness and the unity of all things.

The Shri Yantra is often used as a tool for meditation and spiritual awakening, and is believed to help individuals connect with their inner selves and the divine. It is also used for various other purposes, such as for protection, prosperity, and success in business.

SHRI YANTRA IS A POWERFUL AND INTRICATE SYMBOL THAT REPRESENTS THE BEAUTY AND COMPLEXITY OF THE UNIVERSE, AND SERVES AS A REMINDER OF THE INFINITE POTENTIAL THAT EXISTS WITHIN EVERY INDIVIDUAL.

CHAKRAS

Chakras are energy centers located in the subtle body, or the energetic aspect of the human body, as described in Hindu and yogic traditions. There are seven main chakras that run along the spine, from the base of the spine to the crown of the head.

Each chakra is associated with a specific color, sound, and aspect of consciousness, and is linked to various physical, emotional, and psychological functions in the body. The seven main chakras are:

1. Root Chakra (Muladhara): Associated with the color red.
2. Sacral Chakra (Svadhisthana): Associated with orange.
3. Solar Plexus Chakra (Manipura): Associated with yellow.
4. Heart Chakra (Anahata): Associated with the color green.
5. Throat Chakra (Vishuddha): Associated with the color blue.
6. Third Eye Chakra (Ajna): Associated with the color indigo.
7. Crown Chakra (Sahasrara): Associated with violet or white.

Through yoga, meditation, and other spiritual practices, individuals can work to balance and activate their chakras, promoting overall health and well-being on physical, emotional, and spiritual levels.

AWAKEN YOUR CHAKRAS,
AND YOU WILL AWAKEN THE
INFINITE POTENTIAL WITHIN
YOURSELF, UNLOCKING A
NEW LEVEL OF HARMONY,
BALANCE, AND
CONSCIOUSNESS IN YOUR
LIFE.

MULADHARA
ROOT CHAKRA

Muladhara, also known as the root chakra, is the first of the seven main chakras in the human body. It is located at the base of the spine and is associated with the color red, the earth element, and the sense of smell.

The root chakra is considered the foundation of the entire chakra system, as it represents the grounding and stability that is necessary for all other aspects of life to flourish. It is associated with the basic survival needs of the physical body, including food, shelter, and safety.

When the root chakra is balanced and activated, it can help individuals feel grounded, secure, and stable in their lives. It can also promote feelings of vitality, courage, and resilience. On the other hand, when the root chakra is blocked or unbalanced, it can manifest in physical symptoms such as lower back pain, constipation, or bladder issues, as well as emotional issues such as anxiety, fear, and lack of confidence.

Through various practices such as yoga, meditation, and breathing exercises, individuals can work to balance and activate their root chakra, promoting overall physical, emotional, and spiritual well-being.

BY GROUNDING YOURSELF IN THE STRENGTH OF YOUR MULADHARA CHAKRA, YOU CAN CREATE A SOLID FOUNDATION FOR YOUR LIFE, EMPOWERING YOU TO PURSUE YOUR PASSIONS AND DREAMS WITH UNWAVERING COURAGE AND RESILIENCE.

MULADHARA

root chakra

SVADHISTHANA

SACRAL CHAKRA

Svadhisthana is the second chakra located at the sacral region, near the reproductive organs. Svadhisthana chakra is also known as the "pleasure center" as it governs our sense of pleasure and enjoyment in life. It is symbolized by the color orange and the element of water, which represents fluidity and adaptability.

It is associated with creativity, sensuality, emotions, and pleasure. A balanced Svadhisthana chakra is believed to result in emotional stability, creativity, healthy relationships, and a zest for life.

When this chakra is blocked or imbalanced, it can manifest as emotional issues such as low self-esteem, guilt, fear, and a lack of passion or creativity.

To balance and activate the Svadhisthana chakra, one can practice yoga poses that stimulate the pelvic area, practice mindfulness meditation, use aromatherapy with essential oils like sandalwood and ylang-ylang, and incorporate foods and drinks that support the sacral region, such as orange fruits and vegetables and herbal teas.

BY NURTURING AND BALANCING THE CREATIVE ENERGY OF YOUR SVADHISTHANA CHAKRA, YOU CAN UNLOCK A WORLD OF ENDLESS POSSIBILITIES AND AWAKEN THE PASSION AND JOY THAT LIES WITHIN YOU.

SVADHISTHANA

sacral chakra

MANIPURA
SOLAR PLEXUS CHAKRA

Manipura is the third chakra located at the solar plexus region, near the navel. It is associated with personal power, willpower, confidence, and self-esteem. A balanced Manipura chakra is believed to result in increased confidence, motivation, self-discipline, and a sense of purpose.

Manipura chakra is symbolized by the color yellow and the element of fire, which represents transformation and energy. When this chakra is blocked or imbalanced, it can manifest as issues such as low self-esteem, lack of confidence, indecisiveness, and procrastination.

To balance and activate the Manipura chakra, one can practice yoga poses that stimulate the abdominal area, practice breathing exercises, use aromatherapy with essential oils like lemon and ginger, and incorporate foods and drinks that support the solar plexus, such as whole grains and herbal teas.

MAY THE FIRE OF MANIPURA CHAKRA IGNITE YOUR INNER STRENGTH, EMPOWER YOUR SPIRIT, AND FUEL YOUR PASSIONS TO BRING YOUR DREAMS TO FRUITION.

MANIPURA

solar plexus chakra

ANAHATA

HEART CHAKRA

Anahata is the fourth chakra located at the center of the chest, near the heart. It is associated with love, compassion, connection, and emotional balance.

A balanced Anahata chakra is believed to result in increased capacity for love, empathy, forgiveness, and a sense of interconnectedness with all beings.

Anahata chakra is symbolized by the color green and the element of air, which represents freedom, expansion, and lightness.

When this chakra is blocked or imbalanced, it can manifest as issues such as loneliness, resentment, fear of rejection, and lack of empathy.

To balance and activate the Anahata chakra, one can practice heart-opening yoga poses, practice self-love and forgiveness, engage in acts of kindness and compassion, and connect with nature.

MAY THE LOVE AND COMPASSION RADIATING FROM YOUR BALANCED ANAHATA CHAKRA BE A BEACON OF LIGHT, ILLUMINATING YOUR PATH AND SPREADING WARMTH TO ALL THOSE AROUND YOU.

ANAHATA

heart chakra

VISHUDDHA

THROAT CHAKRA

Vishuddha is the fifth chakra located at the base of the throat. It is associated with communication, self-expression, and creativity.

A balanced Vishuddha chakra is believed to result in clear and effective communication, the ability to express oneself authentically, and a sense of personal power.

Vishuddha chakra is symbolized by the color blue and the element of ether or space, which represents openness, expansiveness, and freedom.

When this chakra is blocked or imbalanced, it can manifest as issues such as difficulty communicating, fear of judgment, creative blocks, and lack of personal power.

To balance and activate the Vishuddha chakra, one can practice throat-opening yoga poses, engage in creative activities, express oneself honestly and authentically, and engage in acts of self-expression.

MAY YOUR VISHUDDHA CHAKRA BE A GATEWAY TO YOUR MOST AUTHENTIC SELF, ALLOWING YOUR VOICE TO BE HEARD WITH CLARITY AND CONFIDENCE, AND YOUR CREATIVE ENERGY TO FLOW FREELY AND EFFORTLESSLY INTO THE WORLD.

VISHUDDHA

throat chakra

AJNA

THIRD EYE CHAKRA

Ajna is the sixth chakra, also known as the third eye, located between the eyebrows in the center of the forehead. It is associated with intuition, perception, and spiritual insight.

A balanced Ajna chakra is believed to result in a strong sense of inner wisdom, clarity of thought, and the ability to connect with one's higher self.

Ajna chakra is symbolized by the color indigo and is associated with the element of light, which represents illumination, knowledge, and insight.

When this chakra is blocked or imbalanced, it can manifest as issues such as lack of clarity, inability to trust one's intuition, and difficulty connecting with one's higher self.

To balance and activate the Ajna chakra, one can practice meditation, pranayama, and visualization techniques, as well as engage in activities that promote spiritual growth and introspection.

MAY YOUR AJNA CHAKRA BE
THE GATEWAY TO A WORLD
OF INFINITE WISDOM AND
INSIGHT, WHERE YOUR
INTUITION AND INNER VISION
GUIDE YOU TOWARDS A LIFE
OF PURPOSE, CLARITY, AND
SPIRITUAL GROWTH.

AJNA

third eye chakra

SAHASRARA

CROWN CHAKRA

Sahasrara, also known as the Crown chakra, is the seventh and highest chakra in the human body. It is located at the top of the head and is associated with the color violet or white. Sahasrara is considered the seat of consciousness and is said to be the gateway to the divine.

The Crown chakra represents our connection to the universe and the divine consciousness that flows through all things. When it is balanced, we experience a sense of unity with all things, and we feel a deep sense of peace and connection to the universe.

Imbalances in the Crown chakra can lead to feelings of disconnection, confusion, and lack of purpose. When the Crown chakra is blocked, we may feel spiritually disconnected or experience a lack of direction in life. On the other hand, an overactive Crown chakra can lead to a sense of detachment from reality.

Meditation, yoga, and other spiritual practices can help balance the Crown chakra, allowing us to access a deeper connection to the divine and a greater sense of purpose and meaning in life.

MAY YOUR SAHASRARA CHAKRA BE THE PATHWAY TO THE DIVINE, WHERE YOUR MIND TRANSCENDS THE LIMITATIONS OF THE PHYSICAL WORLD AND MERGES WITH THE INFINITE CONSCIOUSNESS OF THE UNIVERSE, UNLOCKING THE TRUE POTENTIAL OF YOUR SPIRITUAL JOURNEY.

SAHASRARA

crown chakra

Thank you so much for purchasing my "Yoga Symbols Coloring and Learning Book".
I hope that it brings you joy and relaxation as you explore the world of yoga symbols.

I am always looking for ways to improve and grow, so if you could please leave an honest review of your experience with the book, it would be greatly appreciated.

Thank you again
for your support!

Selah Moon

Printed in Dunstable, United Kingdom

71358471R00051